# PORTO

## THE CITY AT A

MW00860724

### Alfândega

Eduardo Souto de Mo...
customs house into a co...
*Rua Nova da Alfândega, T 22 340 3024*

### Palácio da Bolsa

Take a guided tour of the neo-Palladian stock
exchange, finished in 1910, to ogle the Moorish
revival decadence of the Salão Árabe.
*Rua Ferreira Borges, www.palaciodabolsa.com*

### Clérigos

The tower of Nicolau Nasoni's masterful
1763 church combines baroque exuberance
with the grandeur of a Tuscan campanile.
*Rua de São Filipe Nery, T 22 014 5489*

### Praça da Ribeira

This central square was once a harbourside
market. Now it's a popular meeting place.

### Sé do Porto

Behind the cathedral's imposing facade is a
delightful Romanesque and Gothic interior.
*See p009*

### Hotel Dom Henrique

In 1973, this hotel became the city's first
concrete high-rise. Its asymmetrical shape
recalls Frank Lloyd Wright's Price Tower.
*See p016*

### Ponte Luís I

Gustave Eiffel associate Théophile Seyrig's
1886 bridge seems to fly across the Douro.
*See p013*

### Mosteiro Serra do Pilar

In summer, there are concerts on the terrace
of this 17th-century monastery. The circular
domed church is also worth a visit.
*Largo de Avis-Santa Marinha*

# INTRODUCTION
## THE CHANGING FACE OF THE URBAN SCENE

Portugal's second city is a straight-talking, hard-working town that has always been proud of its mercantile heritage. It is a place of traders and the bourgeoisie and, as a result, there is little by way of grandiose urban set pieces. Indeed, much of Porto's attraction (and its UNESCO World Heritage Site status) derives simply from the manner in which its humble granite houses cluster together picturesquely on the steep terrain. Many of the best contemporary buildings are the signatures of the globally lauded local architect Álvaro Siza Vieira (see p072), whose poetic but deceptively complex modernism is clearly inspired by these dramatic streetscapes.

The city has always been defined by its international harbour, after which it is named. When the port moved out to neighbouring Matosinhos in the 1970s, the centre lost a great deal of its prosperity, and it has taken a long time to bounce back. Now, though, a wave of interest spearheaded by an active arts and student scene has re-energised Baixa with a vibrant cultural life unimaginable only a decade ago. The danger is that the authorities, desperate to clean up the historic old quarters, will scrub out much of their character, destroying a unique environment along the way. For the moment, however, Porto has an old-world vitality and a community spirit that is increasingly hard to find in a major European destination, and a new generation of architects, designers, restaurateurs and artists determined to keep it in sync with the rest of the world.

# ESSENTIAL INFO

## FACTS, FIGURES AND USEFUL ADDRESSES

### TOURIST OFFICE
Porto Turismo
*25 Rua Clube dos Fenianos*
*T 22 332 6751*
*www.visitportoandnorth.travel*

### TRANSPORT
**Airport transfer to city centre**
Line E trains depart every 15 minutes. It's a half-hour journey to Campanhã station
**Car hire**
Avis
*Rua Guedes de Azevedo 125*
*T 22 205 5947*
**Metro**
*T 808 205 060*
*www.metrodoporto.pt*
Trains run from around 6am-1am; the Yellow and Blue lines run 24 hours on weekends
**Taxis**
Raditáxis do Porto
*T 22 507 3900*

### EMERGENCY SERVICES
**Emergencies**
*T 112*
**Late-night pharmacy**
*www.farmaciasdeservico.net*
Check the rota online

### CONSULATES AND EMBASSIES
**British Consulate**
*33 Rua de São Bernardo*
*Lisbon*
*T 808 203 537*
*www.ukinportugal.fco.gov.uk*
**US Embassy**
*Avenida das Forças Armadas*
*Lisbon*
*T 21 727 3300*
*pt.usembassy.gov*

### POSTAL SERVICES
**Post office**
CTT
*320 Praça General Humberto Delgado*
*T 707 262 626*
**Shipping**
UPS
*Rua de José Falcão*
*www.ups.com*

### BOOKS
**Álvaro Siza: The Function of Beauty**
by Carlos Castanheira (Phaidon)
**Hunting Midnight** by Richard Zimler
(Constable & Robinson)
**Journey to Portugal** by José Saramago
(Vintage)

### WEBSITES
**Architecture**
*www.arquitecturanoporto.blogspot.com*
**Newspaper**
*www.theportugalnews.com*

### EVENTS
**Open House Porto**
*www.openhouseporto.com*
**Porto Design Biennale**
*www.portodesignbiennale.pt*

### COST OF LIVING
**Taxi from Francisco Sá Carneiro
Airport to city centre**
€20
**Cappuccino**
€2
**Packet of cigarettes**
€5
**Daily newspaper**
€1.50
**Bottle of champagne**
€80

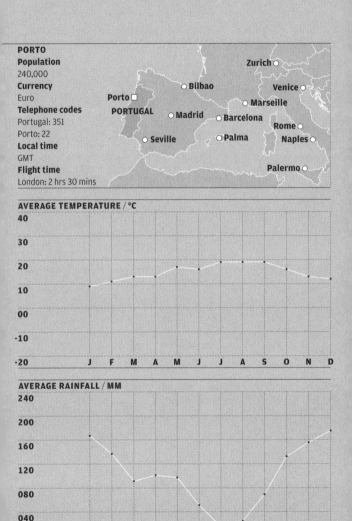

**PORTO**
**Population**
240,000
**Currency**
Euro
**Telephone codes**
Portugal: 351
Porto: 22
**Local time**
GMT
**Flight time**
London: 2 hrs 30 mins

Porto □
PORTUGAL
Seville ○
Bilbao ○
Madrid ○
Palma ○
Barcelona ○
Marseille ○
Zurich ○
Venice ○
Rome ○
Naples ○
Palermo ○

**AVERAGE TEMPERATURE / °C**

40
30
20
10
00
-10
-20

J  F  M  A  M  J  J  A  S  O  N  D

**AVERAGE RAINFALL / MM**

240
200
160
120
080
040
000

J  F  M  A  M  J  J  A  S  O  N  D

# NEIGHBOURHOODS

## THE AREAS YOU NEED TO KNOW AND WHY

To help you navigate the city, we've chosen the most interesting districts (see below and the map inside the back cover) and colour-coded our featured venues, according to their location; those venues that are outside these areas are not coloured.

### MATOSINHOS

The port relocated here to an enormous container facility in the 1970s, though the atmosphere remains sedate. Visit for the top seafood eateries, such as Salta o Muro (Rua Heróis França 386, T 22 938 0870), and to pay homage to architect Álvaro Siza Vieira – his Piscina das Marés (see p074) is a delight – in the place of his birth.

### FOZ DO DOURO

Urbane and leisurely, Foz has long been Porto's sophisticated beach playground. The neighbourhood's wealth is visible in the mansions that line the coastal road and its heavyweight restaurants, such as Pedro Lemos (see p032). However, Foz has been overtaken by Baixa as the city's hippest nightlife and commercial zone.

### BOAVISTA/CEDOFEITA

OMA's Casa da Música (see p010), built on the site of a tram depot, is prominently situated on Avenida da Boavista, a grand 19th-century boulevard that gives this part of town its name. Many of Porto's chicest shops are to be found here, including the menswear gem Wrong Weather (see p094).

### SANTO ILDEFONSO

This residential 'hood rises from the retail hub of Rua de Santa Catarina, yet retains a villagey vibe. Santo Ildefonso is a fine baroque church, but it's the hulking great Silo-Auto (see p014) that dominates the area. Simple *tascas* (snack bars) abound.

### LORDELO DO OURO/SERRALVES

The Serralves Foundation (see p026), with its gardens and contemporary art gallery, is the dominant attraction here, despite its setting amid swathes of monotonous 20th-century housing. Far more appealing is the riverfront, from where the Flor de Gás ferry carries passengers across the water to the pretty fishing hamlet of Afurada.

### BAIXA

Downtown was long considered obsolete in comparison with the affluent suburbs. But since the financial crisis, an effort has been made to reinstate Clérigos, with its steep streets and historic buildings, as the centre of the city's social life. Don't miss the *arrufada* (a sweet bun) at historic café/bakery Confeitaria do Bolhão (see p024).

### MASSARELOS

Once home to the bourgeoisie, Massarelos is still underpopulated and genteel, except for the riverside. Many of its estates were claimed by the state and are now home to university faculties (see p082) and the Jardins do Palácio de Cristal, where you'll find chef Vítor Matos' Antiqvvm (see p088).

### GAIA

Facing Porto from across the Douro, Gaia is famous for its wine cellars, located here as the southern riverbank is less prone to extreme temperatures. East of Ponte Luís I, you'll discover semi-rural housing and the hilltop Mosteiro Serra do Pilar (see p009).

# LANDMARKS

## THE SHAPE OF THE CITY SKYLINE

Maps of Porto give little indication of its harsh topography and sheer cliffs. For the best overview of the city and to establish your bearings, head to the terrace at the Mosteiro Serra do Pilar (Vila Nova de Gaia) for its splendid sweeping vistas. What you will notice immediately are Porto's famous bridges – although the prettiest, Ponte Maria Pia (see p013), will be out of view – along with the central square, Praça da Ribeira, the wine cellars of Gaia south of the Douro and the charming Guindais and Fontainhas districts.

Look for the huge green dome of Pavilhão Rosa Mota (see p083) and follow the skyline east to the baroque tower of Clérigos (Rua de São Filipe Nery, T 22 014 5489), historically used by ships as a beacon, Sé cathedral (Terreiro da Sé, T 22 205 9028), austere from the outside, but with wonderful tiled cloisters, and the Coliseu (see p078), which is a feast of pink and neon at night. City Hall (Praça General Humberto Delgado, T 22 209 7000), a baroque pastiche, is at the top of Avenida dos Aliados, where Portuenses amass in times of both celebration and protest. This boulevard, near the beautiful São Bento station (see p072), forms the civic heart of the city.

Heading away from the centre, the wide Avenida da Boavista, flanked by Casa da Música (overleaf) and Torre Burgo (see p012), leads to the Atlantic suburbs of Foz and Nevogilde, and beyond to the port and seafront district of Matosinhos (see p073).

*For full addresses, see Resources.*

## Casa da Música

OMA's asymmetrical performance hall is spatially rich and materially exuberant, and had a big impact on local architects, not to mention the city itself, when it was opened four years late in 2005. Up until then, Porto's design orthodoxy had been in the Álvaro Siza Vieira mould, but Rem Koolhaas and Ellen van Loon's complex forms and interior detailing – enormous scalloped glass curtains and gold leaf on wood – inspired a new expressiveness. The concrete hulk houses two concert halls, one at the scale of an orchestra and the other more intimate, wrapped in a winding series of circulation and social spaces. Visit the chequered roof terrace and the VIP room, which is a riff on traditional azulejo-tile interiors. *604-610 Avenida da Boavista, T 22 012 0220, www.casadamusica.com*

## Torre Burgo

Eduardo Souto de Moura, a protégé of the Porto School (see p072), has always had a soft spot for Mies van der Rohe; this 2007 Burgo office complex is his lavish tribute. Two buildings, one squat and the other a soaring tower, sit on a podium alongside a sculpture by acclaimed Porto artist Ângelo de Sousa – a typically abstract musing on form and colour. The ensemble is formally simple and internally unremarkable; all the interest is in the facade, which is composed of stacked modules that create repetitive forms, not even disturbed by the entrance, with the glazing deeply recessed. The 70m high-rise is a formidable presence in a part of the city where a clutch of new-builds do little to evoke inspiration, and remains the only significant skyscraper to have gone up near the centre since the 1970s.
*1837 Avenida da Boavista*

### Ponte Maria Pia

Predating the more famous Ponte Luís I, which looms over Ribeira, Ponte Maria Pia is the unmistakable work of Gustave Eiffel, and became the first railway to cross over the Douro when it was completed in 1877. Luís I arrived a decade later, designed by Théophile Seyrig, who was an associate in Eiffel's firm. Maria Pia is the more graceful of the two. The elegantly arched wrought-iron structure was the longest bridge of its kind in the world when it opened. It is only wide enough for a single track but it carried train traffic across the water up until 1991. Since then, it has lain idle. After worrying reports of metal rivets falling off and into the river, the bridge was repaired in 2009, with a plan to open it as a pedestrian and cycle route – unfortunately the idea has failed to gain much traction since.

*Avenida de Gustavo Eiffel*

### Silo-Auto

Porto has never had any qualms about inserting huge car parks into its polite urban fabric; the art deco Maus Hábitos (see p040) dates from the 1930s. João Abel Bessa and Alberto José Pessoa's 1964 Silo-Auto building is a mammoth sculptural cylinder of bare concrete in the rectilinear city centre, a brutalist version of New York's Guggenheim.
*148-180 Rua de Guedes Azevedo*

# HOTELS

## WHERE TO STAY AND WHICH ROOMS TO BOOK

For decades, Porto's finest hotels were located in Boavista and Foz (see p022). However, the revitalisation of Baixa and more recently the quieter well-heeled streets west of it has led to a proliferation of new ventures. Entrepreneurs have radically transformed existing buildings to create design hotels – a pair of pioneering townhouse conversions, Malmerendas (see p019) and Rosa Et Al (see p023), are still popular due to their architectural charm and attention to detail, but now industrial revamps, from Armazém (opposite) to Tipografia do Conto (see p020), are rivalling them for panache.

Meanwhile, long-time favourites, notably the grandiose Infante Sagres (62 Praça Dona Filipa de Lencastre, T 22 339 8500), have had lavish renovations. Vincci (see p036) is set in the 1930s Bolsa do Pescado and public areas make the most out of the old fish market, while themed properties such as Torel 1884 (228 Rua Mouzinho da Silveira, T 22 600 1783) peddle imperial nostalgia. For a business-oriented option, we'd recommend the Sheraton (146 Rua Tenente Valadim, T 22 040 4000), Porto Palácio (1269 Avenida da Boavista, T 22 608 6600) and the well-located, now reborn Dom Henrique (see p038). In Gaia, The Yeatman (Rua do Choupelo, T 22 013 3100) has rooms and a stunning pool overlooking the Douro, but if you really want to escape the urban milieu, head upriver, 20 minutes out of the centre, where Palácio do Freixo (see p098) is hard to beat. *For full addresses and room rates, see Resources.*

**Armazém Luxury Housing**

Locals Pedra Líquida (see p019) renovated a 19th-century iron *armazém* (warehouse) into a nine-room accommodation in 2016. Throughout, exposed stone and untreated wood play off soft furnishings, decorative items from Mercado Loft Store (T 22 616 0951) and light fittings sourced from Coisas da Terra in Sintra. Smart design solutions include a penthouse chest of drawers that doubles as a set of steps leading up to a window in the roof, as well as a refurbished safe employed as a drinks cabinet in the bar. Rusted-iron staircases, built over the original stone ramps, snake upwards from a central patio, one of a few common areas that include a terrace (above). Armazém also rents out three apartments in an old coffee warehouse in Clérigos.
*74 Largo São Domingos, T 22 340 2090, www.armazemluxuryhousing.com*

### Casa 1015

A self-catering property designed by none other than Pritzker prize-winner Eduardo Souto de Moura, Casa 1015 is a singular choice for architecture buffs. It comprises two twin volumes that extend from a pair of intimate interior gardens, and can sleep up to six people. The building is set on a winding street in the well-heeled area of Foz and brings together a host of materials to strong effect – for example, the original stone masonry of the exterior wall makes for a vivid contrast to the smooth concrete annexe. Inside, the rooms are daubed in soft, neutral tones, but the furnishings do feel a little aseptic as a result. However, the slick melding of indoor and outdoor spaces, including verdant suntrap patios, mean we can forgive a little grey here and there.

*1015 Rua Padre Luis Cabral, T 932 650 172, www.casa1015.pt*

### Malmerendas Boutique Lodging

This hotel exemplifies Porto's new breed of boutique accommodation – a classic 20th-century townhouse that still shows off its original features (large windows, wooden floors and decorative structural elements), updated with sleek, Scandi-influenced furnishings. The owners João Almeida and Joana Coelho partnered with architects Pedra Líquida on the five suites, offsetting the building's heritage with homey pieces that conjure up Arne Jacobsen and his ilk. The spacious rooms, each with its own kitchenette, mean that a night or two here feels more like staying in a friend's apartment than a hotel – it is a welcome respite from the city's chains. The Superior King Studio (above) is the pick of the bunch, with a dining area and balcony.
*Rua Doutor Alves da Veiga, T 925 617 444, www.malmerendas.com*

### Tipografia do Conto

Conceived by architects Pedra Líquida, this 10-room bolthole occupies the site of an early 20th-century graphic arts workshop. Embedded in the ceilings and walls are bas-reliefs (B2 Suite Balcony, pictured) inspired by the studio's leftover metal letterpress types. Elsewhere there is gold detailing on salvaged red wood, and glossy white and green azulejo tiles.
*28 Rua de Álvares Cabral, T 22 206 0340*

### Vila Foz Hotel & Spa

Many of this affluent seaside enclave's old stately homes have been either heedlessly restored or left to rot, but Vila Foz stands out in terms of the care taken by architect Miguel Cardoso and designer Nini Andrade Silva in its refurbishment. The seven-suite 1890s manor house (above) is connected to a 59-room new-build via a skylit corridor. The maximalist tendencies on show, like Silva's trippy custom wallpaper, vivid rugs and sculptural fibreglass headboards, are tempered by more conventional inclusions such as dark walnut furniture. Elsewhere, 19th-century bourgeois majesty is on full display in the revamped dining area replete with green velvet drapes and gold stucco, and anchored by an impressive spider-like brass chandelier by local Artur Mendanha. *236 Avenida de Montevideu, T 22 244 9700, www.vilafozhotel.pt*

**Rosa Et Al**

Since architect Emanuel de Sousa and his sister Patricia rescued this three-storey townhouse in 2012, Rosa Et Al has become a hotspot in the city centre, and a hit with Portuenses for its garden brunches and cooking classes. The property features an original domed skylight that crowns a gorgeous staircase, and pieces from Jean Prouvé and Hans J Wegner help complete the difficult-to-obtain feel that the rooms here have hardly been designed at all. The Queen Deluxe City Heritage suite (above) has a huge claw-foot tub and ornamental plasterwork ceilings. The Garden Pavilion, which has a pretty patio, was constructed in 2015. Amenities also offer a homegrown flavour: there are Castelbel bath products, and roaster Vernazza provides the coffee. *233 Rua do Rosário, T 916 000 081, www.rosaetal.pt*

# 24 HOURS

## SEE THE BEST OF THE CITY IN JUST ONE DAY

You could start the day the traditional way with coffee and *pastéis de nata* at cute Confeitaria do Bolhão (339 Rua Formosa, T 22 339 5220). Alternatively, avoid the tourist hordes at the contemporary 7g Roaster (opposite) on the other side of the river, before crossing it on the lower level of Ponte Luís I, for a fine panorama, and then wind your way up to the heart of Porto via the Barredo stairs. It is not an easy city to walk around but it is an exciting one – the oldest part is a labyrinth of alleys, steep inclines and surprising vistas.

The area around Miguel Bombarda is a shopper's delight – the Centro Comercial Bombarda (285 Rua Miguel Bombarda, T 934 337 703), for instance, is an ad-hoc assemblage of retail spaces in which you can find anything from vintage clothes to design objects. Spend the rest of your morning at Fundação de Serralves (see p026). Then, if the weather is good, head to the coast. Catch a taxi to Matosinhos for a leisurely lunch at Casa de Chá (see p028) and a dip in Piscina das Marés (see p074), and stop off at Casa das Artes (see p029) on your way back into town (ask the driver to follow the river for the scenic drive). Finish up in Baixa. Settle in for dinner at Miss'Opo (see p030), or Encaixados (14 Rua Conde de Vizela, T 91 694 5311) for a modern take on *petiscos*, ahead of bar-hopping between happening haunts like Passos Manuel (see p040) and music spot Café au Lait (44 Rua da Galeria de Paris). *For full addresses, see Resources.*

### 10.00 7g Roaster

Tucked behind Gaia's promenade of wine cellars along the Douro, 7g is a great spot at which to begin a day full of superlative views: a short stroll west of here is Porto's UNESCO-protected waterfront, best taken in from ground level. Designed by local firm What's Next Studio, 7g is housed in the shell of a warehouse and boasts a contemporary presence in these ancient back alleys, with light and dark contrasting to great effect inside thanks to Plumen lighting, nets that droop from the ceiling and a liberal use of black paint. Behind a sliding glass door is a lush patio. The speciality coffees are the best on either side of Dom Luís I bridge: Pumpkin Spice Candy is a hit in winter. In the evenings, it also sells Lupum craft beer. Four bijou apartments are for rent above. *52 Rua Franca, T 919 594 606, www.7groaster.pt*

### 12.00 Fundação de Serralves

Not only is this one of the best collections of contemporary art in Portugal, but the estate is worth visiting for its architecture alone. The 1925 mansion by José Marques da Silva is the model of art deco, with its René Lalique skylight, and a neo-baroque chapel that is completely enveloped within the salmon-pink walls, and the landscaping is proto-modernism at its most flamboyant. The museum – which often features large-scale installations such as Olafur Eliasson's 'Y/our Future is Now' – and library, with its Tobias Rehberger ceiling installation, are in a substantial 1999 building by Álvaro Siza Vieira, a sculptural white box in tune with its setting. The lunch buffet at the top-floor restaurant is exceptional, and should be taken on the roof when weather permits.
*210 Rua de Dom João de Castro,*
*T 22 615 6500, www.serralves.pt*

### 13.30 Casa de Chá da Boa Nova

Situated on the rocky coast of Matosinhos, this calm 1963 restaurant was Álvaro Siza Vieira's first major work – and it makes a fascinating comparison with the extension to Serralves (see p027), which was built 36 years later. Boa Nova combines vernacular details, such as the superbly crafted afzelia wood panelling, with a spatial quality that's reminiscent of Alvar Aalto or Frank Lloyd Wright. Have a glass of *vinho verde* (young white wine) in the intimate tea salon before sampling chef Rui Paula's fare (see p096) in the dining room (above), which has long been popular with Portugal's political elite. The two tasting menus (one vegetarian, the other seafood-based) feature dishes such as *à bulhão pato* (clams), and lobster with celery and hazelnut. Pair with suggestions from sommelier Carlos Monteiro.
*Avenida da Liberdade, T 22 994 0066*

### 16.30 Casa das Artes

Located within the grounds of Casa Allen, a neoclassical 1920s pile that was originally built for the Belgian consul to Porto, Casa das Artes was the first large-scale project undertaken by now-starchitect Eduardo Souto de Moura (see p072), and finished in 1991. The cultural venue is understated almost to the point of anonymity from the exterior, its concrete, brick and glass fully integrated into an existing granite wall. The central hall is used for exhibitions, and off it lead two rooms, one reserved for cinema screenings (mainly cult and arthouse) and the other an auditorium for performances by young talent from the Iberian classical music scene. The best time to visit is during the summer season, for alfresco concerts hosted in the idyllic English-style gardens.
*210 Rua Ruben Andresen, T 22 011 6350, www.culturanorte.pt*

### 21.00 Miss'Opo

This café, bar and restaurant occupies the ground floor of a bijou guesthouse (T 932 925 500) and has been pulling a hip crowd since 2011. The decor is a showreel of local design luminaries: delicate pendant lights come from a collaboration between owner Paula Lopes and interior architect Gustavo Guimarães; tableware is from Vista Alegre and Bordallo Pinheiro; and there is also a Scandinavian-influenced cabinet by Piurra

(see p056). Guimarães' aesthetic retains an industrial feel but is warmed by plants and vintage furniture. The unfussy menu might feature ceviche in the warmer months and *feijoada* (bean stew with smoked meat or seafood) in winter. On Thursdays, dessert takes the form of DJs, who spin in the main room as part of the 'sobremesa' events.
*100 Rua dos Caldeireiros, T 22 208 2179, www.missopo.com*

# URBAN LIFE
## CAFÉS, RESTAURANTS, BARS AND NIGHTCLUBS

Porto has always had beautiful cafés, from the belle époque Majestic (112 Rua de Santa Catarina, T 22 200 3887) to the 1950s Ceuta (see p046). The danger of regeneration is that it will erase these slices of history, so it's a blessing that the renovations of Café Candelabro (see p042) and Café Vitória (see p050) have shown the way forward.

Previously, many of the very best restaurants were out near the ocean, and it's still worth the trip to Pedro Lemos (974 Rua do Padre Luís Cabral, T 22 011 5986) and Cafeína (see p043) in Foz, and Casa de Chá (see p028) and the fish grills in Matosinhos. But Baixa is now the heart of the food scene, where chefs elevate the classics with inventive, well-conceived menus, exemplified by Cantinho do Avillez (see p047). Elemento (opposite) and Traça (see p041) do wonders with meat, while a trend for decadent tasting menus big on fresh fish and low on food miles continues, from the high-end O Paparico (2343 Rua de Costa Cabral, T 22 540 0548) in the north-eastern suburbs to the central Semea by Euskalduna (see p035).

It used to be that anyone seeking a kicking night out would have had to jump in a taxi out to one of the peripheral superclubs on an industrial estate. Not any more. Indeed, Baixa has become perhaps too intense at weekends, especially around Rua da Galeria de Paris. For a calmer evening, there are some excellent hotel bars, notably 17° (see p038), and Vincci (see p036), by the Douro in Massarelos. *For full addresses, see Resources.*

## Elemento

Given its elegant setting, it's hard to believe that Elemento is basically a glorified firepit. The food is cooked by flame alone – grilled, roasted or smoked by chef-owner Ricardo Dias Ferreira, who worked in San Sebastián with Martín Berasategui before opening his eaterie in 2019. Sit at the curved bar atop a stool crafted (like the rest of the furniture) by Boavista carpenters to see the action in the kitchen. Though it's all about primitive techniques, the weekly menu is refined and champions local produce: try the lamb loin, which comes with yoghurt and Portuguese *chanfana* sauce. Porto architects Grau Zero used pale wood to play off the 19th-century rough stone walls. A marble-arched alcove showcases the excellent regional wine; we recommend the 2017 Silica unoaked red. *51 Rua do Almada, T 22 492 8193, www.elementoporto.com*

### Pedro Limão

After cutting his teeth in kitchens in Porto, Barcelona, São Paulo and the Algarve, chef Pedro Limão launched his first restaurant, a one-table supper club, in 2010. Additional ventures followed, with this homey 35-seat space opening in 2013. The kitschy art and pastels create a casual vibe, but there is a lot of nous on show in the kitchen, visible from the interior patio, popular with diners in summer. The on-point 10-course tasting menu makes use of organic local produce: choux pastry with shrimp and crab, and the steak tartare with *romesco* sauce are both mainstays. Other dishes, such as aged pork belly, and sweet persimmon, vary with the seasons. Upstairs, there's a guesthouse for non-professional chefs, who get involved in the kitchen during regular pop-up events.
*51-53 Rua do Morgado de Mateus,*
*T 966 454 599, www.pedrolimao.com*

### Semea by Euskalduna

The second project from chef Vasco Coelho Santos following the intimate Euskalduna Studio (T 935 335 301) has been a hit since opening in 2018. Despite its name – which means 'Son of Basque' in Euskera, a nod to Santos' time in Spain – here he commits to using Portuguese produce in sophisticated ways. Try the couvert (semi-cured Azorean cheese with capers, Trás-os-Montes olive oil and rye bread) as well as main dishes such as *açorda* and cod *à la Brás*, and Dom Rodrigo for dessert. Tables left over from a previous restaurant have been sliced and varnished by local firm Atelier MaPa, who also installed Japanese-style pine-and-steel shelving. A piece by Lisbon painter Carolina Piteira anchors the back room (above). As there are only 26 covers, book in advance. *179 Rua das Flores, T 938 566 766, www.semeabyeuskalduna.pt*

### Vincci bar

Architect Januário Godinho's 1934 ocean liner of a building, with its cubist take on art deco, had been left to crumble until the Spanish hotel group Vincci acquired it, entirely overhauling the pile in 2015. Formerly a fish market, a fridge factory, a social centre and a nursery school, it now houses 95 guest rooms, and a roof terrace with views of the Atlantic. But it is the mezzanine lobby bar (above) and ground-floor restaurant 33 Alameda, which serves refined native cuisine, that are the real highlights. Local firm José Carlos Cruz has reinstated a sense of exuberance, and the arched ceilings are offset by sensuous 1940s-style interiors. Be sure to order the house cocktail, which is a potent blend of port, white rum and cinnamon.
*29 Alameda Basílio Teles, T 22 043 9620, www.vincciporto.com*

### Avenida 830

Isabel Neves opened Avenida 830 in 2016. The slender restaurant exudes a casual-chic ambience through neutral tones and minimalist furniture. A lovely rear patio is similarly uniform, anchored by an abstract colour-block wall and concrete fountain. Although Neves has no formal training in a commercial kitchen, she consistently turns out dishes whose good value belie the experimental flavours at play – the swordfish with sweet potato purée and passionfruit dressing is a true revelation. There are the classics too, such as *polvo à lagareiro* (octopus cooked with potatoes and drizzled with plenty of good olive oil). Make this a stop-off after visiting nearby Casa da Música (see p010) and then head on over to Siza Vieira's Bairro da Bouça (see p086), a short walk away.
*830 Avenida da Boavista, T 914 230 462*

## 17° Restaurante & Bar

Though its bar, a local institution, has been open for as long as the 1973 Dom Henrique hotel (see p016) on which it is perched, this 17th-floor restaurant arrived in 2012. Both feature Paulo Lobo interiors that combine plush carpeting, blocky royal-blue seating and geometric gold and copper panelling that adorns the doors and walls. The large windows and plentiful mirrors ensure that the panoramic vistas, which stretch as far as the point where the Douro flows into the Atlantic, are visible to all. Opt for a spot on the dining terrace (above) – the larger of the two decks – for the best views, and try Med fare or national dishes like João do Porto-style cod, grilled octopus with shrimp sautéed in garlic and confit pork cheek with *míscaros* risotto and fig chutney.
*223 Rua do Bolhão, T 22 340 1617,*
*www.decimosetimo.pt*

**Passos Manuel**

This cinema/bar/disco is the handiwork of curator Pedro Gadanho, editor of the provocative architecture journal *Beyond*. Previously a screening room that was part of the Coliseu complex (see p078), Passos Manuel reopened in its own right in 2004. Porto's rising stars of music, art and design compete to stage events here – the kind of alternative and arthouse happenings that wouldn't get a look-in at the Coliseu.

The decor is modern yet also evokes the building's art deco heyday, with a mix of red neon, timber veneer and orange glass. Across the street is Maus Hábitos (T 22 208 7268), a multifaceted venue that comprises a vegetarian restaurant, a bar, a terrace and various exhibition spaces on the fourth floor of a garage that dates from the 1930s. *137 Rua de Passos Manuel, T 22 203 4121, www.passosmanuel.net*

## Traça

Occupying a restored 17th-century building, previously a grocer's, Traça serves classic Iberian comfort food, stylishly plated, and is justly renowned for its superb meat-led dishes. Two must-tries are the boar loin, breaded and stuffed with goat's cheese and foie gras, served on a spread of berry and apple purée; and the Charolais T-bone steak for two, which comes with salad and julienne fries. The open-plan, multi-level space has been warmly refurbished: the ceiling beams have been given a wash of white paint; antlers are mounted on walls; there are antique books, collected by the owners; and the pretty geometric tiling is an inspired touch. This is the perfect spot for a late supper on Fridays or Saturdays, when the atmosphere starts to get lively. *88 Largo de São Domingos, T 22 208 1065, www.restaurantetraca.com*

### Café Candelabro

Ever since the jeunesse dorée rediscovered Baixa, every other shop here looks as if it is a hip nightclub-in-waiting. Although the instinct of many local entrepreneurs is to gut these spaces and start afresh, cousins Miguel Seabra and Hugo Brito took another approach at this beautifully reworked bar, collaborating with architect António Pedro Valente to maximise the character of the 1950s former bookshop – especially the attractive tiled floor – while maintaining a modern edge. Café Candelabro opened in 2009 and draws a sophisticated clientele, who come for afternoon coffee, or a white port with tonic alongside the cheeseboard. Drop by on a Thursday to Saturday night for projections of video art by Portuguese creatives such as Ana Pérez-Quiroga.

*3 Rua da Conçeição,*
*www.cafecandelabro.com*

## Cafeína

Located just a block away from the beach, Cafeína has been *the* neighbourhood spot for Porto's who's who crowd for a couple of decades. The turn-of-the-century edifice is clad in bold yellow-and-black geometric tiles, with the interiors designed by Paulo Lobo, who introduced two elegant spaces: a dining room (above) and an open lounge/bar. In the middle is a curved, darkwood counter that wouldn't look out of place in a 1990s movie by the legendary Manoel de Oliveira. Offering updated Portuguese and European classics, the kitchen focuses on regional fish and seafood. That said, the special carpaccio of beef with foie gras and Ilha cheese isn't a bad place to start. Follow with chargrilled tiger prawns on tagliolini, washed down with a glass of Douro white.
*100 Rua do Padrão, T 22 610 8059, www.cafeina.pt*

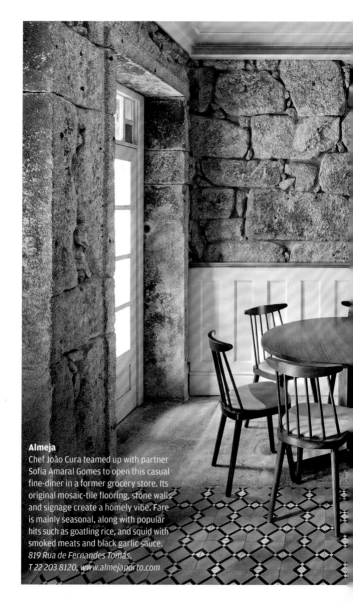

**Almeja**
Chef João Cura teamed up with partner
Sofia Amaral Gomes to open this casual
fine-diner in a former grocery store. Its
original mosaic-tile flooring, stone walls
and signage create a homely vibe. Fare
is mainly seasonal, along with popular
hits such as goatling rice, and squid with
smoked meats and black garlic sauce.
*819 Rua de Fernandes Tomás,*
*T 22 203 8120, www.almejaporto.com*

### Café Ceuta

Once the hip bars currently setting up shop around the town centre have hung up their dancing shoes, no doubt this institution will still be serving quality cups of joe and providing another generation of students and yet-to-be-discovered authors with free wi-fi. The much-loved piece of history from 1953 features a terrazzo-lined coffee house and diner at ground level, with a spacious billiard and games hall below, unchanged since the day it opened. It is the only one of Porto's major cafés to have survived intact. The staff are wonderfully attentive, and the clientele fiercely loyal as a result. There is a sense of postwar optimism about this place that nourishes the soul, making it the after-hours hangout of choice for the discerning Portuenses. In the past it was popular with politicians and ministers. Closed Sundays. *20 Rua de Ceuta, T 22 200 9376*

## Cantinho do Avillez

Chef José Avillez's Cantinho was founded in Lisbon and launched here in Porto in 2014 (his restaurant Belcanto, also in the capital, holds two Michelin stars). The menu boasts fresh variations on home-style favourites: sautéed scallops come with a mushroom risotto, deep-fried green beans with tartar sauce, and cod with breadcrumbs, egg and 'exploding olives'. There are also twists on local specialities, such as its own take on the *francesinha* (a meat-stuffed sandwich that Scooby Doo would be proud of), which Avillez fills with pork varieties and finishes with truffle butter, truffle mortadella and truffle sauce. Architects Anahory Almeida clad the walls in reclaimed wood and added character via charming kitchen items, such as pepper mills and chopping boards.
*166 Rua Mouzinho da Silveira,*
*T 22 322 7879, www.cantinhodoavillez.pt*

### La Bohème Entre Amis

This buzzy coffee spot becomes a chic bar as evening falls. La Bohème Entre Amis is distinctive for its granite facade and wood-and-glass canopy, which draws you inside. It's a natural extension of the interiors, by architects Atelier Veloso, who outfitted the space with a ribbed pinewood framework that unifies its airy three levels. The timber is complemented by simple black-leather upholstered seating, and the many bottles on display. Indeed, the wine list impresses and is exclusively Portuguese, with labels from the Douro to the Algarve. Soak it all up with tapas. We're fans of the *pica-pau*, which here is a deconstructed *francesinha* sandwich presented as a sharing plate, as well as the grilled padron peppers and the sheep's cheese with port reduction. Expect a thrumming atmosphere late on.

*40 Rua Galeria de Paris, T 22 201 5154*

### Taberna dos Mercadores

Many of the new-wave *tabernas* pay lip service to Portuguese culinary traditions without actually imbuing much in the way of substance. But Taberna dos Mercadores, opened in 2014, does not scrimp on either quality or thrills. From the open kitchen comes perfectly cooked dorado, *açorda de mariscos* (the classic bread-based shellfish stew), pork ribs and Arouquesa veal, which are served to just a smattering of tables.

Suffused lighting, a nifty display of wine bottles tucked into the curved ceiling, and an abundance of light wood create a cosy vibe. The visual identity, from the menus mounted on pine to the matching blue-and-white chinaware, was conceived by Porto designers Raquel Rei and Ana Simões. The tavern is popular with those working in the local wine industry, so do book ahead. *36-38 Rua dos Mercadores, T 22 201 0510*

## Café Vitória

This restaurant/café/bar (above) is a big favourite with the after-work crowd. When the weather is fine, do as the locals do and settle into one of the vintage chairs by the likes of António Garcia and José Espinho in the indoor garden (opposite), based in the century-old building's sleek glass-cube extension. Order a top-quality cocktail or craft beer, accompanied by *petiscos* (the Portuguese take on tapas) like red mullet with crème fraîche and miso, and pumpkin terrine with yoghurt. The homey interior is by architect Miguel Tomé, who decorated it with pieces from Pedras & Pêssegos. The upstairs fine-diner serves classic fare with a twist, such as tuna belly with daikon and chicory, all in a lovely setting that features the original wood panelling and tiles.
*156 Rua José Falcão, T 22 013 5538,*
*www.cafevitoria.com*

### Casa d'Oro

Upon its completion in 1963, the Arrábida Bridge was the single longest reinforced-concrete crossing in the world. Legendary civil engineer Edgar Cardoso oversaw its construction from a studio built to his own design and specifications in the bridge's shadow. Now known as the Casa d'Oro, the structure clings limpet-like to the river wall above the Douro, affording stunning views of Arrábida, the estuary and the Atlantic.

Since 2005, the 'House of Gold' has been home to an eaterie run by Italian-born film-actress-turned-restaurateur Maria Paola Porru. Her use of this landmark respects the purity of Cardoso's semi-nautical and semi-cubist concept while maintaining high standards in the kitchen. The tables on the terrace are popular in summer. *797 Rua do Ouro, T 22 610 6012, www.casadoro.pt*

## Portucale

This extraordinary relic of pre-revolution decadence opened in 1969 on the highest floor of the Miradouro apartment block. Many original features remain, from the building's tiled and panelled lobby to the bespoke cutlery on your table. Guilherme Camarinha's fitted tapestries line the walls in an unlikely combination of futurism and Portuguese folklore. Likewise, the dishes, overseen by Ernesto Azevedo's family, are a late-1960s take on national favourites. More modern palates may prefer simpler plates, like the grilled sea bass. Thanks to its position on a hill north-east of the city centre, Portucale lays claim to the highest spot in the city, so the views are excellent. Make a reservation for just before sunset and enjoy the golden panoramas.
*598 Rua da Alegria, T 22 537 0717,*
*www.miradouro-portucale.com*

# INSIDER'S GUIDE

## ESTELITA MENDONÇA, FASHION DESIGNER

Porto born and bred and a graduate of the city's Fashion School, Estelita Mendonça established his menswear label in 2010, sold through Scar-Id (see p095), and he also rates Wrong Weather (see p094) for fashion. He describes his home town as 'curious, a bit dark, a bit melancholy, a very special place' and has witnessed it transform from a sleepy port to a more cosmopolitan destination. 'That contrast of people and stories really appeals to me. It's good for business too – but not so great for finding a place to live.'

His brother is the chef at Camélia Brunch Garden (368 Rua do Passeio Alegre, T 22 617 0009), set by the Douro estuary, and he insists: 'You have to try the eggs benedict and tapioca.' For lunch in town, Mendonça suggests Élebê (37 Rua de Entreparedes, T 22 112 6603), a mini-chain known for its slow-cooked *vitelinha d'avó* ('grandma's veal'). His studio is near versatile Maus Hábitos (see p040), where you can 'see an exhibition, have pizza or coffee, or hang out at the bar'. When he has time, he pops into Mira Galerias (see p067), for its photography exhibitions and cultural events.

For dinner, he flips between old-school tasca O Buraco (95 Rua do Bolhão) and the experimental Euskalduna Studio (see p035). Later, you might find him at sex-turned-dance club Pérola Negra (284 Rua de Gonçalo Cristovão) or eclectic multi-room Plano B (30 Rua de Cândido dos Reis): 'Nightlife here is crazy and exciting.' *For full addresses, see Resources.*

# ART AND DESIGN
## GALLERIES, STUDIOS AND PUBLIC SPACES

Though Lisboetas would never admit it, Portugal's second city has always been more proactive creatively, partly because cheaper rents and production costs have attracted emerging talent from the fields of fashion to furniture, and it is proud of its storied manufacturing tradition. Some of the capital's best art spaces originated here too, including Galeria Quadrado Azul (see p068), Nuno Centeno (see p070) and quirky Ó! Galeria (61 Rua Miguel Bombarda, T 930 558 047), which focuses on illustration, drawing and publishing. Many cluster in 'Bombarda', a scene kick-started when Fernando Santos (see p058) launched in 1993 in this once-quiet residential enclave, which now has more than 20 galleries and a slew of design stores; *inaugurações simultâneas* take place on bimonthly Saturdays. For an overview of contemporary Portuguese art, don't miss Serralves (see p026). It has more than 4,300 works, the main body of which begins 'Circa 1968' (the title of its opening exhibition), through the post-1974 flowering of artistic freedom, up to the present day.

Porto's history as a place of makers, of everything from wine to shoes, has held it in good stead in terms of design. Seek out the handmade furniture by Piurra (193 Rua do Rosário, T 22 094 6101) and the handsome cabinets by Porus Studio (see p060), while Gur (see p061) produces rugs in collaboration with artists and creatives. And then, of course, there's its unique legacy of azulejos (see p066). *For full addresses, see Resources.*

### Culturgest Porto

As at its larger and more active counterpart in the capital, this branch of the Caixa Geral de Depósitos bank puts on regular exhibits. Given its long-time acquisition of big names from Portugal and abroad, shows here are mostly retrospectives of overlooked greats like João Penalva, known for abstract visual storytelling and large-scale installations, and Angela Ferreira, who uses sculpture to examine colonialism and postcolonialism.

In the lobby (above) of the distinctive 1931 building – neoclassical outside, elaborate art deco within – architect Porfírio Pardal Monteiro incorporated Ionic-style pillars to support a double-height octagonal gallery crowned with a stained-glass skylight, and decorated it with marble floors, frescoes, copper details, and wrought-iron doors.
*104 Avenida dos Aliados, T 22 209 8116, www.culturgest.pt*

### Galeria Fernando Santos

A forerunner of the Rua Miguel Bombarda scene, Fernando Santos has been staging impressive shows for about 25 years and is a ground zero for the city's collectors. It represents 40 or so international and Portuguese names – among these, Pedro Calapez, João Louro (*The Portable Kerouac*, pictured, left), Joana Vasconcelos (*Salada de Fruta*, centre) and Pedro Cabrita Reis. *526 Rua Miguel Bombarda, T 22 606 1090*

**Porus Studio**

Established in 2017, Porus blends the best of Portuguese craftsmanship with the spirit of all-American architecture and design, in artisanal, geometric-patterned pieces. The 'Columbia Armoire' takes its cues from LA's grande dame of streamline moderne, Claud Beelman's Eastern Columbia Building, and has an ebony interior encased in brushed-brass with lattice doors. Its shelving system is customisable and can be swapped out to store anything from coats to spirits. The 2m-long 'Hancock Sideboard', inspired by the broody John Hancock Center in Chicago, features dark oak, smoked glass and black leather. Another local company, Piurra (see p056), looks to Europe for its ideas: its Aro range of Bauhaus-style sideboards have a dash of Scandinavian elegance and come with a matte-finished oak or walnut veneer. *www.porustudio.com*

### Senhora Presidenta

Célia Esteves, founder of the artisanal rug company Gur, joined up with three fine arts graduates from the University of Porto to open this gallery/atelier/shop in 2018. The intergenerational match-up paid off, and injected a creative spirit into the touristy centre, through a roster of offbeat events which are by no means limited to drawings on paper (although illustration is the forte here). Gur fits right in. Established in 2013, its limited-edition pieces ('Formiguerio' by Nicolau, above), which can also function as wall hangings, are devised in collaboration with various global artists and designers, from local studio Colönia to Berlin-based João Drumond and Bráulio Amado in New York. They are made from recycled cotton and handwoven in Viana do Castelo.
*65 Rua Joaquim António de Aguiar,*
*T 911 589 193*

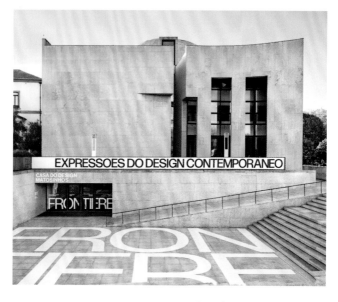

**Casa do Design**

Based underneath Alcino Soutinho's 1987 Matosinhos City Hall in what was intended to be an employee car park, Casa do Design is a joint venture between the council and nearby ESAD (Escola Superior de Artes e Design). Renovated by municipal architects prior to its opening in 2016, one of the old entrance ramps now acts as a gateway to its exhibition space, which hosts between two and three shows per year. Past topics have included a visual history of Portugal's postal service and telecoms industry, and 1960s satirical illustrations, as well as the oeuvre of Álvaro Siza Vieira. Other shows have a far more global reach – 'Frontiere' (opposite), which formed part of the 2019 Porto Design Biennale, shone the spotlight on progressive processes and emerging makers and artisans from all parts of Italy.
*Edifício Paços do Concelho,*
*Rua de Alfredo Cunha, T 22 939 2470,*
*www.casadodesign.pt*

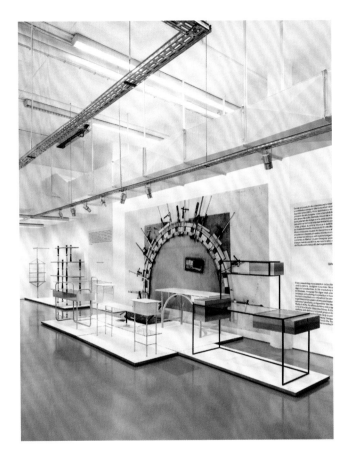

**Kubik Gallery**
Set in Cais das Pedra, on the river west of
the old customs house, Kubik emerged in
2010 as a space to foster the interchange
of culture. Its six shows a year spotlight
up-and-coming artists, mainly based in
Europe (local boy Pedro Tudela's 'Outro';
pictured) and Brazil. Outside the gallery,
a 4 sq m cubicle with a glass door is given
over to guerilla interventions.
*6 Rua da Restauração, T 22 600 4927*

### Quem es, Porto?

Any visitor to Porto will admire the azulejo tiles adorning its buildings, especially the elaborate friezes, like those at São Bento station (see p072). From the early 1950s, a cohort of ceramicists in Lisbon adopted a functionalist approach to the artform; one of the central figures was Maria Keil, whose vibrant 1980s murals zhuzh up the capital's metro stations. Porto-based Júlio Resende (see p079) was very active in the scene; our favourite work is his painterly 1987 *Ribeira Negra*, which spans a wall near Ponte Luís I and depicts tableaux from daily life. A new wave of creatives has taken to the glazed stoneware and begun using it as a canvas. *Quem es, Porto?* ('Who Are You, Porto?'), a collaborative project installed on a facade in the centre of town in 2015, comprises a mosaic of 3,000 hand-painted tiles.
*Rua da Madeira*

## Mira Galerias

A row of 11 abandoned railway warehouses constructed between 1908 and 1917 caught the attention of João Lafuente and Manuela Matos Monteiro in 2016. The pair acquired three, commissioned local architects Floret to restore their cardinal-red doors, granite walls, gabled wood ceilings and Marseille-tiled roofs, and launched them as adjacent art hubs. The first, Espaço Mira, is devoted to contemporary photography in all forms,

with exhibitions often focused on history: Madrileña Gloria Oyarzabal's 'Woman Go No'gree' (above) was an exposé of gender stereotyping in postcolonial Africa. In the other spaces, Mira Forum hosts a diverse programme of performances, screenings and the occasional jazz night, in addition to residencies and solo and group shows. *159 Rua de Miraflor, T 929 113 431, www.miragalerias.net*

### Galeria Quadrado Azul

This pioneering gallery was established in 1986, preceding even Serralves (see p026), and was the first Portuguese venue to show work by Salvador Dalí. Established by the collector Manuel Ulisses, its name means 'Blue Square' and draws inspiration from the futuristic work *K4 O Quadrado Azul*, a satirical pamphlet written in 1917 by the Lisbon agitator and artist José de Almada Negreiros. Besides representing the likes of Álvaro Lapa and Lanhas (both of whom feature in 'L vs L', above), as well as Ângelo de Sousa and Francisco Tropa, it supports students from the School of Fine Arts. It joined the Bombarda crowd (see p056) in 1997; architects Brandão Costa sorted the space into so-called 'moments' (entrance, nave, skylight, exit and courtyard) in 2015. *553 Rua Miguel Bombarda, T 22 609 7313, www.quadradoazul.pt*

### Nuno Centeno

Son of renowned artist Figueiredo Sobral, Nuno Centeno has been influential in the Porto scene since 2007. His gallery's bold reputation comes courtesy of a diverse roster that includes local performance artist and tech pioneer Silvestre Pestana, Mauro Cerqueira, whose multidisciplinary works are rich in social commentary, and Ana Cardoso, a New York-based Lisboeta known for her colourful geometric works.

There are also talents from Brazil and the US – it was the Blake Rayne show 'Carbon Days' that inaugurated this space following Centeno's move from Bombarda in 2018. It publishes single-edition artists' books too. The raw, atmospheric building remains as industrial as it was when it was constructed for the bricklayers' cooperative in 1941.
*598 Rua da Alegria, T 936 866 492, www.nunocenteno.com*

**Mundano Objectos**

Sofia Assalino and Luis Cavalheiro's bijou concept store is packed with a well-edited selection of far-from-mundane objects for practically every part of your home, from books to art, fragrances and fashion, and there's an organic deli too. Global names line the shelves, like French designer Inga Sempé, Naoki Terada from Japan, Dutch talent Hella Jongerius, and the Campana brothers from Brazil. Fans of Scandinavian brands are also well catered for – look out for Hay's 'Uchiwa' lounge chair and Bolia's concrete 'Cemento' bowls. But local items, such as wooden furniture by Mo-ow, Fiu's 'hanging gardens' and eco-friendly clothes by Elementum are worth seeking out. You might go in for some stylish bookends only to emerge with a pair of Aiaiai earbuds. *668 Rua de Santos Pousada, T 916 352 335, www.mundano.pt*

# ARCHITOUR
## A GUIDE TO PORTO'S ICONIC BUILDINGS

Porto is famed for its modernism, largely due to the country's best-known living architect, Álvaro Siza Vieira. His oeuvre ranges from an early domestic refurb that once housed Casa da Arquitectura (582 Rua Roberto Ivens, T 22 240 4663) to social housing at Bouça (see p086) and the geometric tricks of Faculdade de Arquitectura (see p082). His mentor, Fernando Távora, one of the fathers of the Porto School, rejuvenated Palácio do Freixo (see p098) on the city's outskirts late in his career, but his best project is the tennis pavilion at Quinta da Conceição (Avenida Dr Antunes Guimarães). Another alumnus, Eduardo Souto de Moura, gifted Porto the Torre Burgo (see p012), in addition to its entire metro system.

Earlier architecture includes the work of José Marques da Silva, whose 1916 Beaux Arts São Bento station (Praça de Almeida Garrett) has a ticket hall by George Colaço with 20,000 azulejo tiles, the art deco Coliseu (see p078), and Artur Andrade's virtuoso Cinema Batalha (47 Praça da Batalha), an expressive piece of modernism from 1947 wrapped around a 1908 structure, with agitprop reliefs. Once neglected, it's being renovated for 2021. Local practices have taken inspiration from this more playful era, notably Barbosa & Guimarães, whose Vodafone HQ (2949 Avenida da Boavista) has a crystalline form and fine concrete detailing, and Luís Pedro Silva, with a cruise terminal (opposite) that seems to slowly unravel.
*For full addresses, see Resources.*

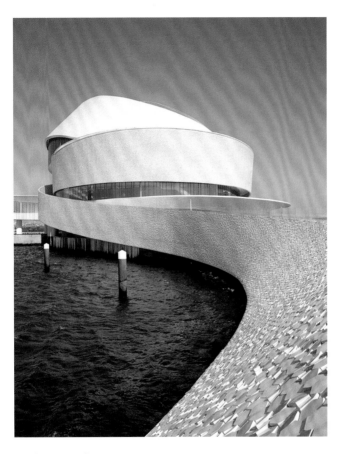

### Terminal de Cruzeiros

The glinting 2015 cruise ship terminal in the port of Leixões, formerly a hub of the fishing and canning industries, is a marker of how Porto's economy is refocusing. The facility accommodates liners up to 300m long and encompasses a marina for 170 vessels. Luís Pedro Silva's building might well be white, following Siza Vieira's great lead, but it differs in its sinuous curves that spin passengers around a bend in the jetty, delivering them out to sea or back to shore. Spiralling ramps envelop the structure like a lazily spooled ribbon, linking functions, guiding circulation and heading up to a rooftop auditorium. The facade is another local tribute, but with a twist – literally, as the hexagonal blocks are angled, evoking barnacles, to reflect the light of the sun.
*Avenida General Norton de Matos, www.apdl.pt*

### Piscina das Marés

One of Siza Vieira's earliest works, which brought him global attention, the 'Pool of Tides' is a profound piece of landscape design on the rocky seafront of Leça da Palmeira, close to his virtuoso Boa Nova teahouse (see p028), also from the early 1960s. From the coastal road, you descend into dark, dramatic changing rooms and emerge to a vista over the granite shore. The swimming areas are artfully carved out of the rocks and supported by concrete walls, allowing bathing in what would be an otherwise inhospitable landscape. There is also a very elegantly composed café and terrace. The unheated pools are open in the summer only and have an eerie feel in the colder months. Since it was unveiled in 1966, the ensemble has inspired architects including Peter Zumthor and Zaha Hadid.
*Avenida da Liberdade, T 22 995 2610*

## Casa da Arquitectura

Local Guilherme Machado Vaz renovated the 1901 Real Vinícola wine factory, with its red-roofed turrets, to house the non-profit Casa da Arquitectura in 2017. The wooden trusses, beams and pillars were rebuilt, the pale yellow plaster facades remade, and the staircases constructed in concrete and positioned outside so as to leave the steel structure undisturbed. Its open spaces are broken up by Porto artist José Pedro Croft's mirrored glass installations, created for the 2017 Venice Biennale. The venue's archive of models, materials, drawings and serigraphs are by leading lights like Siza Vieira, Souto de Moura and Paulo Mendes da Rocha. The core part of the collection covers the period from 1974 to 1999 in 200 projects. *456 Avenida Menéres, T 22 766 9300, www.casadaarquitectura.pt*

### Coliseu

A late art deco landmark with a neon-clad tower, the Coliseu was designed by a team of architects led by Cassiano Branco, and opened in 1941. Inside is a 4,000-capacity concert hall with sweeping galleries, a 300-seat 'attic' room, happening haunt Passos Manuel (see p040) and the Bar Do Coliseu. Everything from the wall reliefs to the light fittings, doors, windows, chandeliers and paintings was custom-made, and the foyer appears untouched since its heyday despite the fact that the building has weathered neglect and a fire, and was almost sold in 1995; it was preserved as a venue only after mass public demonstrations. Another sign of Porto's formidable people power is that it is the cheap tickets (balcão popular) here that are said to deliver the best acoustics.
*137 Rua de Passos Manuel, T 22 339 4940, www.coliseu.pt*

### Igreja de Nossa Senhora da Boavista

The work of architect Agostinho Ricca has been overshadowed by the stellar careers of Távora, Souto de Moura and Siza Vieira, but Ricca also played a major role in the evolution of the 20th-century city. From the early 1960s and through the 1970s, he worked on an estate in the Boavista area, which references Alvar Aalto, Frank Lloyd Wright and Carlo Scarpa. But it was Denys Lasdun who had arguably the greatest influence on this brutalist concrete-and-glass church, built between 1977 and 1981, at the centre of the development. As at Lasdun's National Theatre in London, it displays the timber framework into which the concrete was poured. It is made up of perpendicular strata (overleaf), and has a stained-glass window by Júlio Resende.
*103 Rua Azevedo Coutinho, T 22 600 2691, www.paroquia-boavista.org*

Igreja de Nossa Senhora da Boavista

### Faculdade de Arquitectura

The Porto School emerged in the 1950s as university professors Carlos Ramos and Fernando Távora looked for ways to marry the dictats of modernism with a regional sensibility. After studying here, Siza Vieira followed this approach and would later develop a style that combined high-quality materials, site-generated geometries and white-rendered forms. He came back to teach at the architecture school in spells from 1966 and, naturally enough, was the only choice to overhaul and modernise the campus. Completed in 1994 on a difficult plot – triangular and sloping – he devised a series of pavilions on terraces with the circulation positioned underground. It's a superb example of his work. Seek out his 1980s Carlos Ramos Pavilion, an elegant block at the back of the garden.
*Via Panorâmica, T 22 605 7100*

**Super Bock Arena – Pavilhão Rosa Mota**

Built in 1953 and originally named, simply, the Sports Pavilion, this ambitious project by José Carlos Loureiro is distinguished by its copper-clad reinforced concrete dome, lined with hundreds of circular skylights. It is a grand modernist gesture within the historic landscaped gardens designed by the German Émile David, although many locals preferred the 1865 Joseph Paxton-inspired Palácio de Cristal exhibition hall it replaced. It was renamed Rosa Mota after the local hero and first Portuguese woman to win an Olympic gold, in the marathon at Seoul 1988, but the arena never lived up to this bestowal, and has been mostly used by school teams, and for fairs and exhibitions. However, it was refurbished, extended and given another new moniker in 2019, in the hope of inspiring future generations.
*Rua Dom Manuel II*

### Edifício Soares & Irmão

In the early 1940s, Arménio Taveira Losa was one of many architects proposing a road to connect Avenida dos Aliados with the Palácio de Cristal (see p083). It was thwarted by a huge lump of granite, which proved too costly to move, and the steeply inclined Rua de Ceuta remains as a slice of an unfulfilled urban plan. It is flanked by several Athens Charter-era buildings, including this one for the Soares & Irmão company, designed in 1953 by Losa and his partner Cassiano Barbosa. The Corbusian facade, held on the perpendicular by piloti, is defined by the confident brise-soleil with mobile louvres. Inside, a quite beautiful spiral staircase (opposite), reminiscent of Erich Mendelsohn at his finest, runs up a light well. The building now serves as the offices of Luís Pedro Silva (see p073).
*16 Rua de Ceuta*

**Bairro da Bouça**
After the military coup in 1974, a group of designers formed SAAL, in order to provide decent central accommodation for the working class. Bouça is an estate of 128 townhouses united by a concrete wall that forms three elongated plazas. Not totally finished until 2006, it is now popular with well-heeled buyers seeking a slice of Siza Vieira in a prime location.
*Rua da Boavista/Rua das Águas Férreas*

# SHOPS

## THE BEST RETAIL THERAPY AND WHAT TO BUY

During the noughties, the centre of the city appeared to be doomed as a retail destination, with locals instead heading to suburban megamalls. Perhaps because of this exodus, it has retained a large number of characterful businesses still in their original premises. Of particular note are the labyrinthine hardware shops along Rua do Almada, which is known as the 'street of machines', and the textiles and homewares outlets on pedestrianised Rua das Flores, while Galerias Lumière (157 Rua de José Falcão), a former cinema, hosts unique boutiques, food stops and pop-ups, and 'Bombarda' (see p056) throws up no end of delights for the browser.

Porto's menswear scene is hugely impressive, headed up by La Paz (opposite), and new-wave talent is found in its concept stores, including Feeting Room (see p091) and Scar-Id (see p095). Ladies should head to Pulp Studio (504 Rua do Almada, T 914 763 336) for minimalist jewellery and deconstructed bags and accessories.

The city is, of course, synonymous with port, which is produced in the Douro Valley. Skip touristy Gaia for tastings in the Jardins do Palácio de Cristal at Antiqvvm (220 Rua de Entre-Quintas, T 22 600 0445), and buy from Garrafeira Cleriporto (38 Rua da Assunção, T 22 203 8026). Make your way over to Mercearia das Flores (110 Rua das Flores, T 22 208 3232) to pick up artisan cheeses such as Serra da Estrela and Rabaçal to complete the after-dinner offerings. *For full addresses, see Resources.*

## La Paz

This seriously stylish menswear label was launched in 2011 by André Bastos Teixeira and José Miguel Abreu. The ethos is classic silhouettes with thoughtful craftsmanship, underlined by a smart maritime aesthetic. The flagship occupies a former pharmacy that was popular with sailors arriving at the old docks. It's a touch haphazard but still handsome, with many of the original features, like the bijou cabinetry, having been retained and now sharing space with small interventions by architects Skrei. The brand champions Portuguese production, with most garments made either in Santo Tirso, Guimarães or Barcelos. We picked up the 'Cunha Navy Ecru Logo' sweatshirt and the cotton 'Alegre' shirt, patterned with boats and stocked in spring/summer.
*23 Rua da Reboleira, T 22 202 5037, www.lapaz.pt*

### Matéria Prima

After occupying multiple retail spaces here and in the capital, this paean to Portuguese creativity moved into its basement digs in 2017. Matéria Prima (raw material) started selling experimental music on CD and vinyl in its first bricks-and-mortar shop in 1999 but has gone on to become a fully fledged analogue emporium incomparable to any other store in the city and even, arguably, the Iberian peninsula. Its owner, involved in audio programming and visual arts, stocks everything from exploratory electronica to psychedelic folk-pop from local labels like Crónica and Sonoscopia, as well as Lisbon's Holuzam and Príncipe. There's also a range of editorial oddities – design publications, posters and 'zines – from the likes of Porto printmakers Ana Torrie and Rita Laranja. *127 Rua Miguel Bombarda, T 22 201 1199, www.materiaprima.pt*

### The Feeting Room

Porto shoe manufacturing goes back to the 16th century and entrepreneurs today still favour the city and its surrounds for their high-quality, low-cost leather and labour. But 'Made in Portugal' had been neglected by local retail spaces for a long time, which is why this place made such a splash when it opened in 2015. It features a sharp cast of design and fashion brands, including the likes of C/meo Collective, House of Sunny and Rains, but domestic footwear remains a core focus, seen in hip heels from Gladz, suede boots by Wolf&Son and pastel-hued sneakers from Freakloset, which line the white stone walls of the ground floor. Up the stairs you'll find menswear items and a café that serves baked goods and brews from locals SO Coffee Roasters.
*89 Largo dos Lóios, T 22 011 0463, www.thefeetingroom.com*

### Claus Porto

Ubiquitous in Portugal's apothecaries since 1887, this beauty brand relaunched in 2016 with its own store in the capital, helped out by creative director Anne-Margreet Honing and Achilles de Brito, great-grandson of the man who boosted Claus Porto's fortunes in the 1920s. This three-floor flagship shortly followed suit. The symbiosis of vintage and modern comes courtesy of architect João Mendes Ribeiro, whose bespoke modular cabinets showcase its fragrance and soap lines, which are still handmade in a local factory. A barbershop space at the back is dominated by a polished-brass counter and a marble washbasin (opposite). Upstairs, a charming museum presents the company's visual history and the story of its estate, with past products and packaging labels.
*22 Rua das Flores, T 914 290 359, www.clausporto.com*

## Wrong Weather

Impressive not only for its deconstructivist angled layout, which borrows heavily from the nearby Vodafone HQ (see p072), this lifestyle boutique remains the first port of call for Porto's style-conscious gents. Born out of a collaboration between Joâo Pedro Vasconcelos, CEO of Wrong Design, fashion director Miguel Flor and Lisbon architect Nuno Paiva, it is an all-encompassing retail experience. International brands and the in-house label are on sale alongside music, books and bikes, and there's a mezzanine gallery exhibiting photography, painting and the like. Not far away, over in Clérigos, check out Mercado 48 (T 22 323 9326) for a covetable edit of eclectic locally made items such as glassware recycled from discarded bottles and wooden bicycles by MUD.
*754 Avenida da Boavista, T 22 605 3929, www.wrongweather.net*

### Scar-Id

As a kind of incubator/gallery for selected makers, Scar-Id champions exclusive and limited-run Portuguese products, many of which come courtesy of local artisans and innovators. You might find bold eyewear by Darkside and postmodern leather jewellery by Patrícia Costa along with furniture from Galula, hand-cast ceramics by Lagrima and high-end menswear by Estelita Mendonça (see p054). Owners Sílvia Pinto Costa and André Ramos also put out sleek, minimal homewares and accessories via their own brand, Ater. The showroom boasts bespoke raw-metal display units and a custom two-piece Valchromat desk (above), and hosts events and exhibitions. Scar-Id also runs a space in the back of Casa Vicent (T 22 113 2276), known for its art nouveau facade. *253 Rua do Rosario, T 22 203 3087, www.scar-id.com*

# ESCAPES

## WHERE TO GO IF YOU WANT TO LEAVE TOWN

Porto sits at the mouth of the Douro Valley, and the region has long offered top-quality viniculture tourism from working wineries such as Quinta do Vallado (Peso da Régua, T 25 431 8081), designed by Guedes + DeCampos, and Monverde (opposite) is a vineyard turned luxurious retreat. An hour's drive further east from here is Pedras Salgadas health resort (see p100), where you can bed down in a contemporary tree house. There is also a clutch of restaurants to rival anything in town, including culinary star Rui Paula's DOC (222 Estrada Nacional, Folgosa, T 25 485 8123), located in an elegant structure balanced on stilts in the river by architects Miguel Saraiva. The valley gets more rugged as it nears Spain, and not far from the border is Camilo Rebelo and Tiago Pimentel's 2009 Museu de Arte e Arqueologia do Vale Côa (Vila Nova de Foz Côa, T 27 976 8260), which protects the area's Palaeolithic rock carvings within a brutal but beautifully detailed cantilevered building sliced into a hill.

At the northern limits of Porto's metro, Vila do Conde boasts a 16th-century town centre and aqueduct, and is dominated by the fortress-like Santa Clara convent, although locals flock here for the beaches and nightlife. South of town, Espinho, laid out in a grid, is another seaside escape, with fine art deco architecture. About 40km away is the original Portuguese capital, Guimarães. Its exquisitely preserved medieval core is a UNESCO World Heritage Site.
*For full addresses, see Resources.*

### Monverde, Amarante

The family-run Quinta da Lixa vineyard was transformed into a destination on the Vinho Verde Route (60km east of Porto) with the addition of this carbon-neutral complex in 2015. Architects FCC excavated a hillside and recycled farm structures for materials, and the granite, schist and pine exteriors carry through to an equally well-conceived interior, a collaboration with Paulo Lobo (see p039). Spread through four buildings are 46 spacious bedrooms, a vinotherapy spa with indoor and outdoor pools, a bar and restaurant, and a tasting and 'sensory' room. At its heart, a double-height, sky-lit lobby is hung with Paulo Neves' *Chuva de Folhas*, which comprises 366 carved cedar 'leaves'. You can try making your own wine, ideally as you sample how the experts do it. *Quinta de Sanguinhedo, Castanheiro Redondo, T 25 514 3100, www.monverde.pt*

### Pestana Palácio do Freixo

A good reason to head out to the sprawling eastern suburbs is the Pestana Palácio do Freixo, an 18th-century baroque palace on the banks of the Douro. It was designed by Nicolau Nasoni, the Italian-born creator of many of Porto's greatest civic and religious buildings. In 2000, Fernando Távora gave the grand pile a sympathetic restoration to house the restaurant and bar, as well as a gilded lounge, and gutted the former flour factory next door in order to provide room for 87 elegant accommodations. The pair of buildings are united by an outdoor pool with a sundeck and a landscaped terrace arranged around a fountain that overlook the river. The aesthetic of the hotel block has a somewhat corporate feel – the stars here are the palace itself and the gardens.
*108 Estrada Nacional, T 22 531 1000,*
*www.pestana.com*

**Pousada Mosteiro de Amares, Braga**

Braga, about 50km north of Porto, was a stop-off point for those making the long pilgrimage to Santiago de Compostela in Spain. The legacy of this period lives on in the Bom Jesus do Monte church, reached via a spectacular baroque staircase, and in Santa Maria do Bouro, a 12th-century Cistercian monastery just north of the city. Souto de Moura's superb 1997 overhaul is a sharp lesson in how to transform historic structures to serve new purposes (in this case, the 32-room hotel Pousada Mosteiro de Amares), making the area once again a place of pilgrimage – now for architects and tourists. We couldn't prise ourselves away from the luxe stone-walled environs, but the sporty may consider it a base for exploring the Peneda-Gerês National Park. *Largo do Terreiro, Santa Maria do Bouro, T 25 337 1970, www.pousadas.pt*

**Pedras Salgadas Spa & Nature Park**

Famed for its naturally carbonated mineral springs, Pedras Salgadas has been a health resort since the 19th century. Álvaro Siza Vieira renovated the art nouveau thermal spa in 2009, and it now features an indoor pool bathed in natural light, jacuzzi, sauna, hammam, Vichy shower and 14 treatment rooms. Scattered across the park, 16 eco-friendly accommodation options, designed by Luís Rebelo de Andrade and built from local wood and slate by Modular System, blend into the environment. A pair of Tree (or Snake) Houses (above and opposite) are accessed via ramps that climb up on stilts. Each comes with a kitchenette, bathroom and mod-cons. Elsewhere on site is a mini-golf course, restaurant and museum. Or for more excitement, go rafting on the Douro. *Bornes de Aguiar, T 25 943 7140, www.pedrassalgadaspark.com*

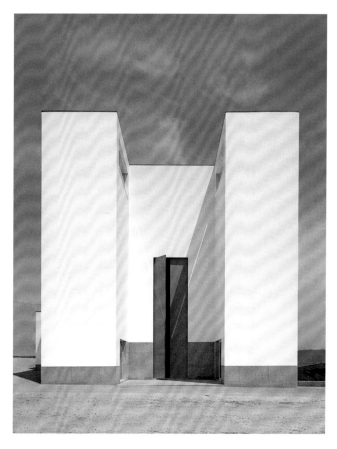

**Igreja de Santa Maria, Tâmega**
Sixty kilometres west of Porto, sat on the fringes of Marco de Canaveses, this 1996 church is among Álvaro Siza Vieira's later works, which are characterised by white marble and render surfaces that decant natural light at varying times of the day, and impeccable levels of craftsmanship. Overlooked by suburban development, Santa Maria's environment is decidedly unpicturesque and the rather grandiose building is not Vieira's most sensitive, but it does command its context. The soaring interior is a sculptural space with a simple off-centre cross; exaggeratedly tall steel doors recall the boldness of Jørn Utzon; and there is a top-lit, tiled baptism area. A congregation of 400 can be seated on wooden chairs designed by Vieira himself.
*Avenida Gago Coutinhos,*
*Marco de Canaveses*

## MIEC and MMAP, Santo Tirso

A 30-minute drive from Porto, the sleepy town of Santo Tirso is home to 57 large-scale sculptures that punctuate its public gardens. The artworks – including pieces by Ângelo de Sousa, Carlos Cruz-Diez and Mauro Staccioli – are part of the Museu Internacional Escultura Contemporânea (MIEC), which received a new HQ (above) in 2016, designed by the dream team of Souto de Moura and Siza Vieira. Beside the meticulously restored 10th-century monastery of São Bento, it is a sublimely minimal, low-slung wing that sits easily within its historic context. Consisting of a café as well as a show space, it shares its entrance with the Municipal Museum Abade Pedrosa (MMAP), which displays regional artefacts across seven rooms of the complex's former guesthouse.

*100 Avenida Unisco Godiniz, T 25 283 0410*

# NOTES
SKETCHES AND MEMOS

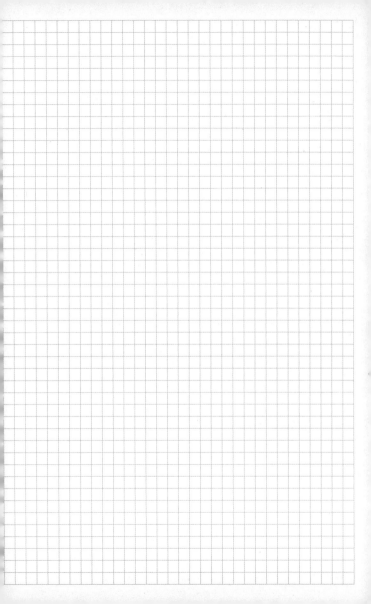

# RESOURCES

## CITY GUIDE DIRECTORY

**A**

**Almeja** 044
*819 Rua de Fernandes Tomás*
*T 22 203 8120*
*www.almejaporto.com*

**Antiqvvm** 088
*220 Rua de Entre-Quintas*
*T 22 600 0445*
*www.antiqvvm.pt*

**Avenida 830** 037
*830 Avenida da Boavista*
*T 914 230 462*

**B**

**Bairro da Bouça** 086
*Rua da Boavista/Rua das Águas Férreas*

**La Bohème Entre Amis** 048
*40 Rua Galeria de Paris*
*T 22 201 5154*

**O Buraco** 054
*95 Rua do Bolhão*
*T 22 200 6717*
*o-buraco.negocio.site*

**C**

**Café Candelabro** 042
*3 Rua da Conceição*
*www.cafecandelabro.com*

**Café Ceuta** 046
*20 Rua de Ceuta*
*T 22 200 9376*

**Café au Lait** 024
*44 Rua da Galeria de Paris*
*www.cafeaulait-porto.blogspot.com*

**Café Vitória** 050
*156 Rua José Falcão*
*T 22 013 5538*
*www.cafevitoria.com*

**Cafeína** 043
*100 Rua do Padrão*
*T 22 610 8059*
*www.cafeina.pt*

**Camélia Brunch Garden** 054
*368 Rua do Passeio Alegre*
*T 22 617 0009*

**Casa da Arquitectura** 076
*456 Avenida Menéres*
*T 22 766 9300*
*www.casadaarquitectura.pt*

**Casa da Música** 010
*604-610 Avenida da Boavista*
*T 22 012 0220*
*www.casadamusica.com*

**Casa das Artes** 029
*210 Rua Ruben Andresen*
*T 22 011 6350*
*www.culturanorte.gov.pt*

**Casa de Chá da Boa Nova** 028
*Avenida da Liberdade*
*T 22 994 0066*
*www.casadechadaboanova.pt*

**Casa do Design** 062
*Edifício Paços do Concelho*
*Rua de Alfredo Cunha*
*T 22 939 2470*
*www.casadodesign.pt*

**Casa d'Oro** 052
*797 Rua do Ouro*
*T 22 610 6012*
*www.casadoro.pt*

**Casa Vicent** 095
*T 22 113 2276*
*www.vicentporto.com*

**Cantinho do Avillez** 047
*166 Rua Mouzinho da Silveira*
*T 22 322 7879*
*www.cantinhodoavillez.pt*

# HOTELS
## ADDRESSES AND ROOM RATES

**Armazém Luxury Housing** 017
Room rates:
double, from €180
*74 Largo São Domingos*
*T 22 340 2090*
*www.armazemluxuryhousing.com*

**Casa 1015** 018
Room rates:
two people, from €130;
four people, from €180;
six people, from €230
*1015 Rua Padre Luís Cabral*
*T 932 650 172*
*www.casa1015.pt*

**Infante Sagres** 016
Room rates:
double, from €170
*62 Praça Dona Filipa de Lencastre*
*T 22 339 8500*
*www.hotelinfantesagres.pt*

**Malmerendas Boutique
Lodging** 019
Room rates:
suite, from €110;
Superior King Studio, from €140
*Rua Doutor Alves da Veiga*
*T 925 617 444*
*www.malmerendas.com*

**Miss'Opo Guesthouse** 030
Room rates:
double, from €70
*49 Rua de Trás*
*T 932 925 500*
*www.missopo.com*

**Monverde** 097
Room rates:
double, from €90
*Quinta de Sanguinhedo*
*Castanheiro Redondo*
*Amarante*
*T 25 514 3100*
*www.monverde.pt*

**Pedras Salgadas Spa & Nature
Park** 101
Room rates:
Eco House Deluxe, from €180;
Tree House, from €210
*Bornes de Aguiar*
*T 25 943 7140*
*www.pedrassalgadaspark.com*

**Pestana Palácio do Freixo** 098
Room rates:
double, from €170
*108 Estrada Nacional*
*T 22 531 1000*
*www.pestana.com*

**Porto Palácio** 016
Room rates:
double, from €100
*1269 Avenida da Boavista*
*T 22 608 6600*
*www.hotelportopalacio.com*

**Pousada Mosteiro de Amares** 099
Room rates:
double, from €100
*Largo do Terreiro*
*Santa Maria do Bouro*
*Amares*
*Braga*
*T 25 337 1970*
*www.pousadas.pt*

**Rosa Et Al** 023
  Room rates:
  double, from €170;
  Queen Deluxe City Heritage, from €200;
  Garden Pavilion, from €290
  *233 Rua do Rosário*
  *T 916 000 081*
  *www.rosaetal.pt*
**Sheraton** 016
  Room rates:
  double, from €120
  *146 Rua Tenente Valadim*
  *T 22 040 4000*
  *www.sheratonporto.com*
**Tipografia do Conto** 020
  Room rates:
  double, from €140;
  B2 Suite Balcony, from €150
  *28 Rua de Álvares Cabral*
  *T 22 206 0340*
  *www.casadoconto.com*
**Torel 1884** 016
  Room rates:
  double, from €150
  *228 Rua Mouzinho da Silveira*
  *T 22 600 1783*
  *www.torelboutiques.com/torel-1884*
**Vila Foz** 022
  Room rates:
  prices on request
  *236 Avenida de Montevideu*
  *T 22 244 9700*
  *www.vilafozhotel.pt*
**The Yeatman** 016
  Room rates:
  double, from €260
  *Rua do Choupelo*
  *T 22 013 3100*
  *www.the-yeatman-hotel.com*

## WALLPAPER* CITY GUIDES

**Executive Editor**
Jeremy Case

**Author**
Syma Tariq

**Photography Editor**
Rebecca Moldenhauer

**Art Editor**
Jade R Arroyo

**Senior Sub-Editor**
Sean McGeady

**Editorial Assistant**
Josh Lee

**Contributors**
Emma Kalkhoven
David Knight
Daniëlle Siobhán Mol
Eleanor Trend
Rachel Ward

**Interns**
Freya Anderson
Alison Evans
Hannah Makonnen
Alex Merola

**Porto Imprint**
First published 2011
Third edition 2020

ISBN 978 18386 6114 4

**More City Guides**
www.phaidon.com/travel

**Follow us**
@wallpaperguides

**Contact**
wcg@phaidon.com

**Original Design**
Loran Stosskopf

**Map Illustrator**
Russell Bell

**Production Controller**
Gif Jittiwutikarn

**Assistant Production
Controller**
Lily Rodgers

**Wallpaper* Magazine**
161 Marsh Wall
London E14 9AP
contact@wallpaper.com

Wallpaper*® is a
registered trademark
of TI Media

**Phaidon Press Limited**
Regent's Wharf
All Saints Street
London N1 9PA

**Phaidon Press Inc**
65 Bleecker Street
New York, NY 10012

All prices and venue
information are correct
at time of going to press,
but are subject to change.

A CIP Catalogue record for
this book is available from
the British Library.

# PHOTOGRAPHERS

**Nelson Garrido**
7g Roaster, p025
Pedro Limão, p034
Semea by
Euskalduna, p035
17º Restaurante & Bar,
p038, p039
Almeja, pp044-045
Estelita Mendonça, p055
Culturgest Porto, p057
Senhora Presidenta, p061
Casa do Design, p062, p063
Mira Galerias, p067
Nuno Centeno, p070
Casa da Arquitectura,
pp076-077
Matéria Prima, p090
Scar-ID, p095

**João Morgado**
Casa 1015, p018
Malmerendas Boutique
Lodging, p019
Rosa Et Al, p023
Casa das Artes, p029
Miss'Opo, pp030-031
Vincci bar, p036

Avenida 830, p037
Traça, p041
Cafeína, p043
Cantinho do Avillez, p047
La Bohème
Entre Amis, p048
Taberna dos
Mercadores, p049
Café Vitória, p050, p051
Kubik Gallery, pp064-065
Quem es, Porto?, p066
Mundano Objectos, p071
Piscina das Marés,
p074, p075
La Paz, p089
MIEC and MMAP, p103

**Roger Casas**
Porto city view,
inside front cover
Casa da Música, pp010-011
Torre Burgo, p012
Ponte Maria Pia, p013
Silo-Auto, pp014-015
Fundação de
Serralves, p027

Casa de Chá da
Boa Nova, p028
Passos Manuel, p040
Café Candelabro, p042
Café Ceuta, p046
Casa d'Oro, p052
Portucale, p053
Coliseu, p078
Igreja de Nossa Senhora da
Boavista, p079, pp080-081
Faculdade de
Arquitectura, p082
Super Bock Arena -
Pavilhão Rosa Mota, p083
Edifício Soares & Irmão,
p084, p085
Bairro da Bouça, pp086-087
Wrong Weather, p094

**Bruno Barbosa**
Claus Porto, p092

**Fernando Guerra**
Monverde, p097

**Duccio Malagamba**
Igreja de Santa Maria, p102

# PORTO

## A COLOUR-CODED GUIDE TO THE HOT 'HOODS

**MATOSINHOS**
The main harbour was moved to this beautifully rugged stretch of coast in the 1970s

**FOZ DO DOURO**
Wealthy Portuenses have always made their homes where the Douro meets the Atlantic

**BOAVISTA/CEDOFEITA**
The Casa da Música concert hall is a must-see and the nearby boutiques are top-notch too

**SANTO ILDEFONSO**
This delightful residential district comes as a surprise so close to the bustling Downtown

**LORDELO DO OURO/SERRALVES**
One of the top contemporary art collections in the country draws the crowds to Serralves

**BAIXA**
The old town is a joy to explore and its steep lanes are home to hip bars and restaurants

**MASSARELOS**
Architectural gems here include Pavilhão Rosa Mota and Siza Vieira's university buildings

**GAIA**
Cross one of Porto's many bridges for spectacular city views and its legendary wine caves

For a full description of each neighbourhood, see the Introduction.
Featured venues are colour-coded, according to the district in which they are located.